DOWN WITH POETRY!

DOWN WITH POETRY!

Helena Nelson

HAPPENSTANCE

By the same author:

How (not) to Get Your Poetry Published, HappenStance 2016
Plot and Counter-Plot, Shoestring Press, 2010
The Unread Squirrel, HappenStance, 2009
Unsuitable Poems, HappenStance, 2005
Starlight on Water, Rialto Press, 2003

Thanks to the editors of the following publications where some of these poems, or earlier versions of them, first appeared: *Ambit, Disquieting Muses, Obsessed with Pipework, PN Review, Snakeskin, Smiths Knoll, The Poets' Republic,* and *The Rialto.*Some poems in the first two sections previously appeared in *Unsuitable Poems* and *The Unread Squirrel.*

I am grateful to Marcia Menter for unsuitable advice.

First published in 2016
by HappenStance Press
21 Hatton Green, Glenrothes KY7 4SD
www.happenstancepress.com

ISBN: 978-1-910131-36-7

Paperback edition printed and bound in the UK
by Martins the Printers Ltd, using acid free paper
sourced from mills with FSC chain of custody certification
www.martins-the-printers.com

CONTENTS

Unsuitable Poems

Mrs N Enters the Literary World / 9
Self-Portrait as an Unsuitable Poem / 10
And Then I Woke Up ... /11
Blind Date / 12
Self-Portrait as the Song of Solomon / 13
Eight Tips for New Poets / 14
Thumbscrew / 15
Self-Portrait as an Eighteenth Century Stanza / 16
The Fucking Vernacular / 17
Emidepic / 18
Poetry Virgin / 20
Like / 21
Mr Kiss / 22
Leap Year / 26
Coming / 27
Peeing Song / 24
Voiced / 25
Self-Portrait as Two Lines by Stevie Smith & Four Lines
    by Emily Dickinson / 26
Poetry Forum / 27
Pickle / 28
Bellytalk / 29
Falling in Love / 30
Warning / 31

More Unsuitable Poems

Thus Far / 35
Pomophobe / 36
Squirrel / 37
Obit / 38
Submission Guidelines / 39

How to Piss Off Your Prospective Poetry Publisher / 40
Literary Taste / 41
Poetry Mobile / 42
The Poetry Publishing Carol / 44
Finding the Time / 47
In Praise of Vers Libre *or* Let the Strain Take the Train / 48
Ending / 50

Anti-Poetry

Prepositions / 53
The Inaugural 'Not On The Short List Prize' / 54
At the Poetry Reading / 56
Precipice by M.Q. Devine / 57
Rant / 58
Fillers / 60
Reasons to be Grateful for Your Ms Not Having Been Returned
by Faber & Faber after Thirteen Months / 62
Acolytes / 63
Performance Poem / 64
What Not to Write on the Back Jacket of Your Debut Collection / 68
Managing Your Expectations / 69
The Contemporary Poem Explains Itself / 70
Performance Poet's Rag / 71
The Poet's Role / 72
On Obscurity / 73
The Poem That Does /74

About the Author

UNSUITABLE POEMS

Dear Helena,

Many thanks for the poems. These aren't quite suitable, but you have a distinctive voice, and you probably have some or will write some that are (suitable). Do subscribe (special offer at the moment) …

[Magazine rejection slip, 2004]

Mrs N Enters the Literary World

I know it's hard to believe me when I say
(watch my lips)
I once found it hard to get my poems published.
I used to get—Rejection Slips.

In those days the little magazines
—sole recipients of my writing—
clearly needed waking-up—
their editors were uninviting.

As time went by I grew more bold—
no doubt I was inspired by The Muse.
I won elevation by a device
which happily transformed their views.

The purchase of a Wonderbra
which I wore to a poetry slam in Fife
at the cost of £19.99
was the single thrust that changed my life.

I took two poems, short and sweet
and pinned one neatly to each cup
and then I raised my cleavage up,
dangling the poems in mid-air,
suspended like Parnassus where
my readers (those abreast) could stare.

And thus it was a genre started,
my coup de bra, my magnum opus
shared by my sisters (try and stop us.)
The world of Arts Review and Crit
refers to us—we're not part of it—
with quiet reverence as—Lit Tit.

Self-Portrait as an Unsuitable Poem

The proper kind of poetry
has resonance—it's heavy.

Her verse is light, the critics said,
she writes it on the bevvy.
She writes the stuff, they said, all night—
we should impose a levy.

A penalty to sort her out.
A sonnet to constrain her.
A job attending funerals.
A way of sounding saner.

Unlace her rhymes. Unscan her shoes.
Can *someone* not restrain her?

And then I woke up...

You were extremely red in the face
and when you opened your mouth to speak
you made no sense at all, you were obviously pissed
first thing in the morning and I told you so.
Did you care? No.
You said they had slipped something into the soda water,
                                        it wasn't your fault
and in any case you were never drunk before nine o'clock I knew
                                        that perfectly well
and then because of that—obviously—
I had to marry the man who picks up litter round here, the one
                                        with the funny hat.
I didn't want to do this because, as I told him,
I didn't think marriage was a great idea and in any case
he was already married and had six children
but he just laughed and it turned out he was
the editor of a poetry magazine called *Trash*
and he told me not to be so stupid because I was only dreaming
and so I woke up except I was still dreaming
and in the dream I had woken up and was writing a poem
about the dream, another dream poem
for Kevin's magazine *Trash*
and it was going to be wonderful, like no other dream poem
had ever ever been, and then I woke up
and bugger me—*is* this a poem?

Blind Date

I'm sweet. I'm petite. I can rave. I can groove.
Hung-over just slightly but really don't show it.
This little red dress is snug as a glove.
I just hope they don't fix me up with a poet.

Mascara. Tiara. Blusher. High heels.
A wild oat remaining and ready to sow it.
Let's hope he'll have money. Let's hope he'll have *wheels*—
but let me not end up in bed with a poet.

No noting, no quoting, no 'wrote you a poem'.
A speedy rapport with no line-breaks to slow it.
No name-dropping (Paterson? met him? I *know* him).
Dear God, please remember, I don't want a poet.

Self-Portrait as the Song of Solomon

I am freckled, but comely,
   O ye daughters of Caledonia,
     as the smooth side of a fresh trout
    as the stippled flesh of a barbecued salmon.
Look not upon me, because I am freckly,
   because my genes are Celtic genes.
      My mother's family were angry with me;
   because I went away to Scotland;
     but mine own country have I not kept.
A motor mechanic is my well-beloved unto me;
   he shall lie all night in our double bedroom.
My beloved is unto me as a fragrance of diesel
   in the fuel tank of an Audi.
Behold, thou art fair, my love;
   behold, thou art fair in thy red boiler suit.
Behold, thou art fair, my beloved,
   yea, my treasure:
     also our bed is king-sized.
The roof of our conservatory is glass
   and our garage non-existent.

Eight Tips for New Poets

1. *Read modern, current verse*
Byron, Blake, Burns in the bin.
Ancients out, Armitage in.

2. *Subscribe to two or three good quality small press magazines.*
What dreams may come? But here's the rub:
they will not print poems in exchange for your sub.

3. *Join a Writers' Group.*
Consult the Poetry Society to see if there is one in your area.
If there is none, it is scary. If there is one, it is scarier.

4. *If you use traditional forms, do it in a new way.*
For several hundred years the sonnet has stayed the same
because nobody dared change it.
Rearrange it.

5. *Create an audience for your work.*
Practise reading poems aloud.
Invite friends round. Dispense drink. Read to the assembled crowd.
Retire upstairs to your study, unbowed
but bloody-minded.

6. *Win a National Competition.*
If you're hesitating whether to win or wait,
win. Don't hesitate.

7. *Write your name and address on every sheet submitted; but not © Hugh Snowball.*
The former is professional & subtly revealing.
The latter suggests you are pompous & regard your poems as worth stealing.

8. *Do not submit your poems with a eulogistic letter citing previous publications.*
If your work has Merit, the rest is history.
(How so much garbage is printed every month while yours is returned
is a mystery.)

Thumbscrew

Poetry bores me.
I think I will become a poet
so I can bore people.

Inflicting boredom's not so far from pain.
I have always been interested in pain.

I had never thought of poetry like this
until now. I am less bored than I was.
I think dinner can wait.

I have written a lovely poem about a thumbscrew.
Let me show you my new metaphor.

Self-Portrait as an Eighteenth Century Stanza

This Poem's life is very sage and still.
Withouten fuss opinion is convey'd.
Ye other Poems, do thou what you will;
And wander through sestinas in the shade
Of complications pointlessly essay'd:
Let each as likes her best her hours employ
While I make satyre on the current trade.
Since Wit dwells here, unfashionable ploy,
She little Praise expects who others doth annoy.

The Fucking Vernacular

'Fuck aye, gie me fower fried eggs fer starters
but fuck sake, mither—nae fuckin mushrooms.
An pooer me some tea—hot as fuck.

Pass me the fuckin ketchup, feyther.
Fuck—fuck—it's no cummin oot.
Thick as shit in the neck ay a bottle.

Fuck this looks guid. Fuckin fantastic.
Fuck knows hoo ahm this fuckin hungry—
fuckin famished.'

An fer ower five meenits
he shuts the fuck up.

*

Emidepic

The woman on the news said there was
'an emidepic racing out of control'.
I was completely faniscated
though faniscation quickly led to fear
and fear, in turn, to panic.
What kind of emidepic did she mean?
And could I be—no, surely not—
fatally conmatinated?
Had I caught it from the radio?
And how could that be pobissle?

The illness sounds lucridous, I know,
but life goes on.
I have learned to live with the flaw
in my brain's right hespimere.
Doctors so far have failed to alanyse
the cause, although the disease
edivently gets in through the ears,
causing a radiply accerelating elovution.
The thing can start
with a tiny consufion in *just one word*.

The damage is mafinested thus:
two likely connosants reverse.
We call this 'connosantal shift'
(not *un*like connitental drift)
and as a conquesence, some say
the words acquire a certain freshness,
even charm. Don't get drawn in—
not for one moment. Language
is willing slave to meaning—
all else is padory.

I know what you are thinking:
It will never happen to me.
Well, here is an ancient redemy
just in case. To wit:
ulitise each day one thousand simple words—
short ones—arappently the hesphimere
reverts. (Poets and nolevists, forget it!
Liretary enveadour requires liretary vobaculary
—though in the human breast,
hope springs enertal.)

Poetry Virgin

The Onboard Customer Service Team
welcomes you to this poem.
There is a pause provided at the end of most lines
and at the end of every stanza.
We apologise for the absence of rhymes.

A quiet stanza is situated near the rear of the poem
for readers who do not like howling.
Passengers should familiarise themselves
with the safety exits
and the lay-out of the poem.

Due to problems with signalling devices
the message of the poem has been somewhat delayed.
We apologise for the delay
but recommend the scenic views from stanza four
and the excellent wordplay in the buffet.

The Customer Service Team wishes to reassure travellers
that this poem is equipped with the latest enjambment
and is not a sonnet of the Petrarchan variety.
If you have any cause for discomfort,
write, please, to the Poem Mistress at Barking.

The poem is due to arrive at its destination
in approximately one
                              minute.
                                        Please
make sure you take all your belongings with you
and nothing that does not belong to you.
Thank you for travelling Poetry Virgin.

Like

I was like *Read this poem*
He was like *You must be joking*
I was like *Pleeeease*
He was like *Fancy a drink?*

I was like *Get lost*
He was like *I really like you*
I was like *Read this poem then*
He was like *Do I have to?*

I was like *Yes*
He was like *Omigod she means it*
I was like *Shutupandreadit*
He was like *Gimme the poem*

       * * *

I was like *Did you like it?*
He was like *What was that about?*
I was like *What did you think?*
He was like *It was like, like …*

I was like *That's the point*
He was shocked, like.

Mr Kiss*

He promised me a load of bliss.
He said he'd make me Mrs Kiss.
'So tell me what this Bliss stuff is,'

I said. A little look of dread
bedewed his brow. 'Get in the bed.
The proper bliss is when you're wed

but what you are about to get
is next best thing,' he said. I let
him talk me into something wet

and rather sudden and—oh dear—
there was a kind of atmosphere
of something not quite happening near

the business end of things. I missed
the point where bliss occurred and this
I pointed out to Mr Kiss

who said I was ungrateful. 'Bliss
is rarely savoured by a Miss
but always by a Mrs. This is

(hand on heart) what Mrs Kiss
insists, in fact the firm basis
of our marriage.'
                              'Ah, you rat—desist!'

I cried. He'd lied. I wasn't ready
for this. He'd said we were going steady
only to get me into bed. He

also said that my frigidity
needed a man of his rigidity
and should we try again? Stupidity

was certainly his forte. 'No,'
I said. 'This fumbling come-and-go
has no bliss in it.' Funny though—

I called his wife at half-past five.
Bliss was it then to be alive
but to get even, very heaven.

*The Rialto Winter Competition 2004 invited entries on the theme of *Bliss* suitable for reading at a wedding ('Short poems … for those whose loving hearts have found their home'). 'Mr Kiss' was not short-listed.

Peeing Song

I frequently pee in the shower.
More often I pee in the bath.
Outside on the ground when there's no-one around
I pee and I pee and I laugh.

On occasion I pee on the hearth rug,
then scrub it and wash it and boil it.
When mother is here we are very austere
and both of us pee in the toilet.

My cousin pees daily when drinking green tea—
she does the whole thing with élan.
Like a fountain she pees and with great expertise
insists that she pissed in the pan.

My granny's gone off to Ohio
where people call lavatories 'John'
Let's hope that they hold quite a lot—I am told
her bladder is second to none.

I pee when the moon is ascending
or when my silk underwear nips;
I pee with huge might in the depths of the night
and during each solar eclipse.

I pee when I'm writing my poems:
they begin with a 'p' and they end
with an 's' like the hiss of a wee that has missed
or a flush that has gone round the bend.

Voiced

Rumpkins is a new voice in poetry.
She tweets sweetly.

If Stan Pip is the Mini Cooper of Voice,
Witters is Rolls Royce.

Twaddle has lost his voice, and found it—twice.
Voice is his vice.

Mopmore has finally found her voice.
She is PBS-recommended choice.

For Dumpty, voice is less voice than VOYSE
i.e. lots of noise.

Bendiqueep has a distinctive voice:
a whiff of Woolf; a hint of Joyce.

As for the voice of Dai Blenerys—
it is *sui generis.*

Voice is everything in poetry. Voice is It.
All else is technique or witless wit.

Self-Portrait as Two Lines by Stevie Smith & Four Lines
    by Emily Dickinson

This foolish woman thinks her Muse will spout
Real poetry. But her Muse has gone out.

       * * *

Form cannot confuse—
It firms the line that strays—
Wait a moment—I'll put on—
My momentary—stays—

Poetry Forum

'What is poetry for?' (Maitreyabhandu)

It's for weddings
and funerals
and reading on the train
and for taking a person out of herself
and bringing her back more sane.

It's for children
and lunatics
and chimney-sweeps and punks
It's for teachers
and preachers
and politicians and drunks.

It's for dinner
and afternoon tea
and marvellous midnight snacks.
It's for cravings
and ravings
and low-poetry attacks.

It's for four o'clock
for four of us
and for five o'clock
for five.
It's for fortitude
and forums
for formalists to survive.

It's for all we know intelligent
and rarely less than clever.
You can get some
for nothing
and remember it
forever.

Pickle

I have all the latest significant poets
pickled, seasoned and clearly ordered.
They look very well in jars,
silently alphabetical, each accorded

equal respect. I keep the shelves neat
and—as for vinegar—only the best.
The seals are perfect,
even though noses are pressed

(in some cases pleadingly) against the glass.
It is, of course, for the expert to gauge
which of them will just seep in pickle juice,
which will improve with age.

Bellytalk

Last night your stomach spoke to me again. At first just a gurgle, like before, then a sudden groan. *I don't think I can bear much more*, it said, *of this modern verse you make me swallow. Prose-poems make me want to puke, daren't say this when head's awake.* I gave your leg a kick but your hard neck muscled in. *It's not the imagery*, it said—*it's the content. One more poem about Alzheimer's and I'm off.* There was a quiver from your buttocks. *Want to know what we think?* they asked. No, we all replied in italics. Quickly I got up to brush my teeth.

Falling in Love

I didn't believe in falling in love
until I fell in and couldn't get out.
I didn't even have time to shout—
I lost my footing, lost my nerve,
shot head-over-heels down the endless curve
of the helter-skelter some call *lurv*.

You're sixty-five and your hair is thin.
Your polo shirts do not hold mystique
and I am not rich or blonde or chic.
I had no idea it would all begin
with your anxious, apologetic grin
and outstretched hand—but I pulled you in.

It's dark in here, little sense about,
just soupy songs about me and you
and all the revolting words are *true*.
I'm in lurv with you and in pain without:
they'll write on our headstone, not much doubt,
Fell in, silly sods, and couldn't get out.

Warning

The train may be longer than the platform.

The platform may be shorter than the train.

The poem may be longer than your patience.

This one stops here.

MORE UNSUITABLE POEMS

Thus far

Too many poets. Clustering, crawling, crowding, climbing,
scraping the last clouds off the sky,
sucking them into wet spit balls
                    and pinging them at us.
Noisesome creatures.

Enough.

Pomophobe

After Mrs McFarlane's class
I discovered I was pomophobic.
I've never liked poems much
or aerobics.

It was like the poem was a bird with its beak clamped shut
on a worm.
We had to force it open with an essay
written at home.

I got it out in one piece
but practically threw up in prose.
Mention the word *poem*
and I vomit. Here goes.

Squirrel

Note: I was recently commissioned not to write a lengthy narrative poem titled as above, and since the offer was financially advantageous I accepted. The poem would have highlighted (in 54 ottava rima stanzas) the pressure that the red squirrel—SCIURUS VULGARIS—has been under from the grey squirrel—SCIURUS CAROLINENSIS—for several generations in lowland Scotland. The invitation not to write the poem was based on a strong belief on the part of the commissioner that my poem might encourage further aggression from the greys—actually, so to speak, egging them on. I concede that any grey squirrels reading the poem would have been emotionally affected by it, perhaps even angered. The poem, however, is lost to posterity. A single epigram remains.

When I think of him, my senses birl—
The subtext grey, the unread squirrel.

Obit

The title was *Copacetic.*
'To K.S.' below it.
Four hundred lines, and three made sense.
He was a poet's poet.

Submission Guidelines

Do not go gentle into that villanelle.
Allow yourself a period of remission.
Rage, rage against a rhyming hell.
Why they exist, no laureate can tell

but certain writers choose them. Bad decision.
Do not go gentle into that villanelle.
You have a talent? Use the talent well.
You owe the world a lesser imposition—

rage, *rage* against a rhyming hell.
Oppose Verse Torture.
What sadist could compel
this agony of tedious repetition?

Do not go gentle into that villanelle.
Try analgesics. Anything to quell
the lethal urge. Recite this admonition:
Rage, RAGE against a rhyming hell.

The form is dead. Attend its passing bell.
Bury the bastard. Sue for demolition.
Try a sestina. Forget that villanelle!
It's not too late, it's really not. Oh well.

How to Piss Off Your Prospective Poetry Publisher

How shall I tell you? So many ways.
Under-stamping is not the worst: nice people do it
unintentionally. Perhaps first of all you should
disregard the possibility that there may be
Submission Guidelines. If, however, you find any,
ignore them. Present your work in a font
slightly too small for the publisher to read
comfortably, or vary the size and type of print
from page to page so as to maximise
the flotsam-and-jetsam effect. Use punctuation
here and there. Staple the poems together
without remorse. Number every page.
Tell the publisher you have written over 500 poems
since last March. Never mind about your address but do
display your name at the foot of each poem
prominently, preferably with a copyright symbol
to prevent the publisher stealing your work
and passing it off as her own. Do not sign
your letter. Instead, type (below the space where your signature
is not) J. Smith/Jones/Heaney etc: POET.
No need to enclose an S.A.E.—so old-fashioned
when editors should reply by email.
Include a link to your website and a four-page CV
listing every poem you have ever had published,
no matter where (or when). Do not read
any of the publisher's current list to ascertain
whether your submission will harmonise
or shout NO NO. Make time
to ensure the last two lines of your poems rhyme
even if all the rest do not. Include as many
villanelles/sestinas as you can. Invite the publisher
to read more about you, on your website. Don't
forget to mention the novel,
the one you are writing at this moment.

Literary Taste

In love with Briskit I am not. I do not care for him.
His ways are wild, his tongue is loose,
his syntax somewhat grim.

In love with Lumpitt? Maybe so. His style is rarely grand
but I admire his reckless mix
of and and &.

In love with Matt until I die I am, indeed I am
but I have not forgotten you
or new blackcurrant jam.

Poetry Mobile

Welcome to Poetry Mobile.
We value your poem.
Please hold on
while we try to connect you.

Thank you for your poem.
Your poem is held in a queue.
All of our editors are < *busy* >
Please hold on

or contact us via the website
at poetrymobile.com.
Thank you for your patience.
Your poem is now in a short-list.

Please call back the short-list number
during working hours.
Welcome to Poetry Short List!
Please key in the title of your poem

while we try to connect you
the title of your poem
should not exceed < *twenty-three digits* >
Welcome to Poetry Short List!

You have made it to the last
< *one hundred* > poems
All of our editors are < *counting* >
Please call back.

Welcome to Poetry Short List!
You have made it to the last
< *fifty* > poems.
All of our editors are < *dizzy* >.

Please call back.
Welcome to the Short List of
< *ten* > poems!
Thank you for holding.

Your poem is important to us.
All of our editors are < *dead* >.
Thank you for calling
Poetry Mobile.

The Poetry Publishing Carol

(to be sung to the tune of & etc)

The first time I tried it, I sent my poetry
To Picador (Paterson, D.)

The second time I tried it, I sent my poetry
To Carcanet
And to Picador (Paterson, D.)

The third time I tried it, I sent my poetry
To Enitharmon,
To Carcanet
And to Picador (Paterson, D).

The fourth time I tried it, I sent my poetry
To Faber, yes (& Faber),
Any Enitharmon,
Carca-carcanet
And to Picador (Paterson, D).

The fifth time I tried it, I sent my poetry
To Waterloo,
To Faber, yes (& Faber),
Any Enitharmon,
Bust a Carcanet
And to Picador (Paterson, D).

The sixth time I tried it, I sent my poetry
To Chatto, oh and Bloodaxe,
Halloo Waterloo,
To Faber, yes (& Faber),
Any Enitharmon,
Lost a castanet
And to Picador (Paterson, D).

The seventh time I tried it, I sent my poetry
To Arrowhead and Eyewear
Chatto, oh and Bloodaxe,
High Waterloo,
To Faber, yes (& Faber),
Any Enitharmon,
Philip Larkinet
And to Picador (Paterson, D).

The eighth time I tried it, I sent my poetry
To Diehard and to Luath,
Arrowhead and Eyewear,
Chatterblow and Mud-axe,
To you Waterloo,
To Faber, yes (& Faber),
Any Enitharmon,
Tarka the Otter
And to Picador (Paterson, D).

The ninth time I tried it, I sent my poetry
To Nine Arches Press,
To Diehard and to Luath,
Arrowhead and Eyewear,
Chatteroo and Mud-axe,
Woo-hoo Waterloo,
To Faber, yes (& Faber),
Any Enitharmon,
Narky Carcanet
And to Picador (Paterson, D).

The tenth time tried it, I sent my poetry
To Cape and Smith Doorstop,
Nine Arches Press,
To Diehard and to Luath,
Arrowhead and Mywear,
Chatterbling and Mud-axe,
Blue Peter Loo,

To Faber, yes (& Faber),
Any Enitharmon,
Fishnets and suspenders
And to Picador (Paterson, D).

The eleventh time I tried it, I sent my poetry
To Flambard, Arc and Shearsman,
Cape and Smith Doorstop,
Nine Arches Press,
To Diehard and to Luath,
Arrowhead and Highwear
Champing at the Bit-axe,
Stew Waterloo,
To Faber, yes (& Faber),
Any Enitharmon,
Noah's Arcanetta
And to Picador (Paterson, D).

The twelfth time I tried it, I sent my poetry
To Cinnamon Drop Siren,
Flimsy Mark (a Salesman),
Stuff the Back Doorstep,
Nine Itches Press,
Diehard with a vengeance,
Barrowboy and Eyesore,
Battleaxe and Chancy,
Lose Waterloo,
Toss the old Caber,
Any Thermal Stockings,
Get me on the net
And to Dickador (Paterson, D).

The thirteenth time I tried it, I made my poetry
A self-publication.
Guess who
Is publishing
Me?

Finding the Time

It isn't easy. I have to search
all the places I searched before,
fighting the fear it isn't there

until I encounter a thimbleful
between a button still not sewn
and the not-yet-planted flowering currant

behind our shed with the leaking roof
beside the path with the broken stones
at the end of the day which (oddly) is made—

like the gingerbread house—
of all that I need.

In Praise of Vers Libre or Let the Strain Take the Train

I had a human brain.
I left it on the train.
Now all I've got is rhythm and the rhythm is insane.

I'm jamming like an email which has lost its 'from' and 'to'.
I haven't got a subject line. I haven't got a clue.
I want to stop this nonsense and I *would* sound more like me
if something wasn't missing where my brain's supposed to be.

I had a human brain.
I left it on the train.
Now all I've got is rhythm and the rhythm is insane.

I don't remember what I wrote before I lost the plot.
It might have been forgettable but then again might not.
It might have been exceptional and won the Forward Prize.
It might have got me on TV. But—try this out for size:

I had a human brain.
I left it on the train.
Now all I've got is rhythm and the rhythm is insane.

There's gotta be a simple way to counteract this crap.
I never met a rapper who was trapped inside a rap.
Perhaps I'm haunted. Some dead poet (out to take the piss)
is forcing every line I write to manifest—like this:

I had a human brain.
I left it on the train.
Now all I've got is rhythm and the rhythm is insane.

I could be very lonely—if from now to kingdom come—
I'm stuck with *tumpty-tumpty-tumpty-tumpty-tumpty-tum.*
What *did* I do to merit this unenviable fate?
I saw a nice psychiatrist. She said it was Too Late.

I had a human brain.
I left it on the train.
Now all I've got is rhythm and the rhythm is insane.

There *is* a way! There is! Oh yay! It's come to me this minute.
It's like a relay baton and I pass the rhythm in it
to someone unsuspecting who's prepared to win the race
while I write proper poems at a proper poem pace.

I had a human brain.
I left it on the train.
Now all I've got is rhythm and the rhythm is insane.

Guess who? It's you. It's *you,* my friend. Oh feel the sudden flood
of rhythm in your fingertips and rhythm in your blood!
The energy's phenomenal. The pleasure's almost pain.
You've got it, haven't you? Yes, yes—you've got it. Take the strain:

You had a human brain.
You left it on the train.
Now all you've got is rhythm and. . .

Ending

He betook himself to a wood
but the wood wasn't a wood
and the logs were sleeping like people
and the trees were thick as thieves.
He'd stolen away and was glad
to go in, and inside In.
It's just thee and me, he said.
With my glad rags on, he said.

ANTI-POETRY

Prepositions

After Stevie Smith

Pity this poet, she is underestimated,
she undertakes long poems and they are underrated,
all of this under the reign of Queen Elizabeth the Second to whom
she is not even distantly related.

Lo! the road to Parnassus should not be forsaken
for here is a poet who has overtaken
many front-runners, we call him Rover
because he wins the National Poetry Competition over and over.

I like to read Mrs Between,
she is neither one nor the other, she has often been
between a Black Rock and a bard place,
nevertheless her verse is lean.

O look! this nice young man is moving up to the Next Generation,
we must run upstairs with a sense of elation,
up up up like an escalator,
perhaps we will catch up with this creator.

Alas, poor Miss G, aged thirty, is wearing a frown.
She applied for a Gregory and was turned down
and she goes down-down-down to the bottom slopes
where she is down-market, and eventually elopes.

Afterword:
Post (as in post-modern) means 'after'—
post-avant (after-before in French) is considerably dafter
but these poets are always after something.
They did not vote for Brexit. Hark to them singing:
O Salutaris Hostia! If we had stayed, and switched to the Euro
all of our poems would be worth more-o!

The Inaugural 'Not On The Short List' Prize

My book didn't win the Costa Award
so it comes as no surprise
to find it is not on the shortlist
for the Seamus Heaney Prize.

It is not the Saltire Book of the Year
and ineligible for Wales.
The Forward Prize for best of its size
is numbered among its fails.

It was entered for T.S. Eliot
and the Roehampton Poetry Prize,
and (in manuscript) for the Anthony Hecht
that Waywiser organise.

I didn't expect it to soar to fame
because I'm not published by Cape
(or Picador, Bloodaxe or Carcanet)
but I somehow expected to scrape

into a shortlist somewhere,
a group of worthy non-winners.
I am not, after all, a member
of 'Poetry For Beginners'.

So I'm launching a prize of integrity
not in the least like the rest—
for poets of valour and fibre
prepared to be put to the test.

The NOTSL award is strict but fair.
To demonstrate aptitude
you must list the noteworthy journals
in which you have not been reviewed;

and your record of competitions
will demonstrate how you have been
NOT on a shortlist for several awards
(no fewer, let's say, than thirteen)

with proof that you actually entered
and a book with poems within.
The shortlist for NOTSL will be quite long
and everyone on it will win

gold stickers: 'Shortlisted for NOTSL!'
(to put on their book's front jacket).
The poetry racket's for crack-pots—
it takes a true crack-pot to crack it.

At the poetry reading

Lambasted. It's no use.
I've shut my ears. I'm done.
I'm sitting here, but darling
I have gone. *Gone.*

'Precipice' by M. Q. Devine

A: Poetry is boring. I don't understand it.

B: Most poetry is boring. But this is different.

A: It's just the same as all the rest.

B: No, really. Look what it says on the jacket—*Exciting and new.*

A: I don't understand. You said it was poetry.

B: It's *exciting* poetry. It takes risks.

A::   What kind of risks does it take?

B: New, exciting risks.

A: I don't understand.

B: Risks of style and form. On page 23 it almost

                                        fractures meaning.

A: It does what?

B: Read it. You'll see.

A: I won't understand it.

B: You may not understand it. But you'll *like* it.

A: I don't like things I don't understand.

B: But it's *exciting* and *new.*

A: You're just saying that to get me to read it.

B: No I'm not.

A: Yes you are.

B: Yes, I am. You're missing so much.

A: Is it funny?

B: No.

A: Is there a story?

B: Not exactly.

A: Boring.

B: Exciting. New. *Invigorating.*

A: Invigorating how?

B: It will fill you with energy.

A: You said it was poetry.

B: It is invigorating poetry.

A: Please go away now.

Rant

Down with poetry! It's all over the place,
clogging up the drains, pretending
to be special. It's printed on demand,
when there is no demand. Bookshops
don't want it but still it gets printed. There are
poems in broadsheets and pamphlets
and hardbacks and paperbacks
and postcards and posters—
all of them rubbish! Bag it and bin it!
Who can understand it? Half of it
doesn't make sense, the other half
doesn't want to. Nobody knows how to read it. Oh
they pretend they do, but they haven't a clue.
Apart from at funerals, what is the point of it?
It doesn't even rhyme, or it rhymes,
which is worse. There are magazines
with pages full of nothing but poems
and articles about poets and letters from poets
about poems and poets. They are all mad.
Delusion, delusion—
the confusion of profusion. Give me
a small piece of perfect prose
any day of the week. Down with
bluff and puff and blurb and bluster!
Down with performance and festivals!
Down with clamour and slammers
and *Best Of* anthologies! Down with 'débuts'
and longlists and shortlists and prizes!
Down with Winning Poems! Down with podcasts!
Down with young poets and old poets
and permanently middle-aged poets,
and poets who think their poems will sell!
Down with chopping sentences

into stanzas—especially couplets! Down with poets
who marry, or cohabit and breed—
down with their seed! Get them off the radio
and into a job. Down with payments for poets
to teach poets to write poetry! (Why
encourage them?) Down with 'mentors'
and Creative Writing degrees! Down with
List Poems and Found Poems and National Poetry Day!
Down with workshops! Down with poems with 14 lines
that say they are 'sonnets'! Down with iPads
and Facebook and Twitter and Instagram and YouTube!
Down with networking! Down with the internet!
Down with what they haven't even thought of yet
but will be the Next New Thing!
Down with the Muse!

Bring back twenty years between collections.
Bring back TB. And garrets. And bedlam. And capital
letters at the start of every line.
And meaningful punctuation. And flogging
for blogging. Bring back quill pens and blotting paper
and astronomically expensive ink. Bring back scansion
and writing half the time in Latin
on tombstones. Bring back dead poets.
Bring back parchment. Bring back embarrassment.
And—for persistent po-fenders and recidivists,
villanelle and sestina producers,
poetry promoters, poetry patrons, poetry peddlers,
poetry piss-artists and poetry publishers—
bring back writer's block!

Fillers

(BADABUM is a drum roll or similar. It stands in place of where a poem might have been at a reading. Effectively this poem is made up of the 'fillers' between four poems, although the poems themselves aren't actually delivered.)

I *um*
am fascinated by rhythm *um*
by the way the rhythm of what poets *um*
say between the poems differs *um*
from the way they speak the poems. It's the *um*
nowhere space, in between one poem *um*
and the next *um*

speaking of which my next poem *um*
is just a short one and *um*
I am not going to read it

BADABUM BADABUM

because here I am dealing with the between 'ums' *um*
the 'ums', the lang lumbs between the crumbs *um*
of wisdom. Recently I *um*
developed a theorem *um*
which says that there are two types of poet—there are 'ummers' *um*
and 'er-ers' *er*

I go on to suggest—and this is more risky—*um*
that 'ummers' are female *um*
(it's a mum sound 'um'—a female phoneme *er*
whereas 'er' is a male, father figure) *er*

but after extensive study I have conceded that some men *um*
are ummers (bummer). This next poem *um*
is about some of those men *um*
who become trapped in the 'um' continuum *um*
but I'm not going to share it

BADABUM BADABUM

because what I want to do here *um*
is to hover, to hover between uncertainties *um um*
sacrificing nothing to your expectation of immediate resolution *um*
you could say I am at the point where the 'ums' *um*
and 'ers' *er*
get in the poem's way. A conundrum.

BADABUM BADABUM

But hey—the possibility has not escaped me that *um*
the poem itself (the one I haven't read yet) might be *um*
crap. So I'm not going to read the *um*
poem which should have followed this filler, although *um*
after all this *um*
it certainly would have seemed more of a poem *um*
than it otherwise might.

Reasons to be grateful for your ms not having been returned by
Faber & Faber after thirteen months

1. It is a privilege for paper you have touched to be touching
    the surface of a desk or drawer or filing cabinet at Faber & Faber.
2. Faber & Faber did not reject your poems the same week you
    sent them.
3. The idea of being published by Faber & Faber is delightful
    and continues to be accessible to you.
4. You can tell your friend and publicist: 'My ms is with
    Faber & Faber.'
5. You can use this period of hiatus to make 'working towards
    a second collection' a reality.
6. The sense that you don't exist is a creative opportunity.

Acolytes

They hung on his every word,
some of them like wet washing,
others like corpses.

Performance Poem

Sorry: this is going to be complicated
and you will need to concentrate.
Although this is called 'Performance Poem'
I (the poet) am not the one performing.
You are performing the poem,
at least that's what I hope you will do.

I intend to ask you to employ
the body language of poem-response,
something you may never consciously
have thought about until now.
Please humour me, even when you sense
an absence of actual poem.

It is widely accepted that
specific experiences result in specific responses.
Recent research, however, (Paterson and Hollis, 2011)
indicates that where the body responses
are mimicked, the emotions that might
have given rise to them (but did not)
start to be experienced.

Let me give you an example:
people who feel happy often smile
but smiling (even without the associated
feeling of happiness) cheers people up—
they have endorphins to prove it.

So this poem, or poem notion, on which
you are currently concentrating, as requested earlier,
will require you to mimic the body language
of response to a poem—to act out,
as it were, the process of listening

to a poem in live performance.
In this way, you will experience
the remarkable benefits
of a first-class poem without actually
having to listen to one.
Please follow the instructions.

1.

At the start of the poem-listening experience
there is the business of perking up and,
so to speak, pricking the ears.
A slight tenseness about the shoulders: the body
is on the alert, on the *qui vive*, as the poet
begins to speak the opening line.
Please perk up *now*.
(You may find your jaw is slightly clenched
as though you are ready to bite.)

2.

Good. Hold that position while
the poem (or in our case the notional poem)
proceeds. You will need
almost to nod your head.
The head inclines slightly, so one ear harkens,
as it were, to the source of
sound, and the chin lifts.
The harkening ear actually points
towards the poet
as the head almost nods
and the brain responds
line by line
by line by
line by
line.

Well done. Continue like this
for at least twenty imaginary lines.

(It will not surprise you to learn that
the body language of poetry response
is massively understated: one small sniff
is worth sixteen stanzas.)

3.
Now. The poem is building. It is building to a climax.
This requires you to lean forward slightly—
but not too much, it will disconcert your neighbours
if you have any. Now you are communicating
a sense of anticipation and risk.
(Risk, because you know the poet
may have created false hope and so
you haven't wholly committed yourself
in case the poem turns out to be bollocks.)

4.
The dénouement is approaching:
take a short quick breath, hold it, hold it, hold . . .
preparing yourself, preparing yourself,
preparing for the AHA moment: *aaaaaaaaaaaaaaah*
and release the breath. Very good.
That was also an epiphany

5.
and it leads almost immediately to
the moment of closure. Relax the shoulders,
sit back, breathe evenly, let the creases
on your forehead un-crease, your mouth drop
into a weak smile. Un-grit your teeth
and relax your jaw.

The poem is about to end, it is going to end,
it is ending it is ending NOWWWWwww w w w.

6.
The poem has ENDED
and you are still processing that thought
and as you process it, you feel moved to vocalize
a tiny *hmmm*. That's it. *Hmmmmmmmmm*
and it's just loud enough to hear
as the *hmmm* swells and swells until
it gradually fades and as it fades
it creates its own beautiful
answering
si . . . lence.

7.
As much as you like,
as loud as you like—
CLAP.

What Not to Write on the Back Jacket of Your Debut Collection

This book is not bad.
A number of these poems feature the poet's dog: George.
The author's mother recommends this book.
Boris Johnson recommends this book.
Most of the poems are quite short.
Poetry is not for everybody.
These poems are accessible if reasonable adjustments are made.
Many of these poems were written while dusting.
The poet applied three times for funding to assist in the completion
of this book.
Please buy this book.
The poems in this book have universal resonance some of the time.
Includes five villanelles and three sestinas.
There is a glossary of difficult words for readers new to poetry.
The poet skilfully employs seven types of metonymy.
The main theme is death.

Managing Your Expectations

This poem won't do
what you expect it to
though in the end
I suppose it does depend
on what you expect.
I'd like to protect
the art of the obscure
and the feeling of somehow wanting more
while not quite knowing more
of what.

Well?

Did it?

The Contemporary Poem Explains Itself

I'm not allowed adjectives and adverbs.
Exclamation marks are out too, which is sad.
I can have any amount of verbs, I adore verbs.
My tone is casual, but that's just a front.
I do my thing mainly in the present tense
and I'm almost always justified
except when I'm all over the place.
I long to be understood, but I worry
about being understood too easily.
I'm often, but not always, thin. (I don't have to be thin.)
Show not tell is my mantra. (I am against mantras.)
Repetition still works in my book
but epiphanies are off the menu and not likely
to be back this year, no need to brace yourself.
I have tried to do without line breaks
but sometimes they mean
everything (that was a cheap trick, sorry).
I feel safer in stanzas, especially when they're linked by
that thing nobody's really comfortable
saying out loud—*enjambment*—
and I do worry about the origin of any word
connected with legs which it is, yes, from the Middle French
enjamber: 'to straddle or encroach on'.
Well-planned encroachment is fine, though frankly
you can over-straddle.
I am aware I used two adjectives on the line before the one before this one.
Right. You're supposed
to go back to the beginning now
and get to know me better.

Performance Poet's Rag

Oh-oh, oh-oh
what draws folk to me so?

It isn't my money
cos I don't got any.

It's probably not my looks
or my cooking of my books.

Guess it isma
charisma.

The Poet's Role

The poet's role, as we shall see,
is to challenge established authority.
The poet's role is to take control.

The poet's role is to undermine
the assumptions of the asinine.
The poet's role is to be a mole.

But the poet's role has been overstated.
Statisticians have estimated
how miserably thinly the role is spread.
They say it's the worst thing since sliced bread.

On Obscurity

They're shy, and often difficult.
Clarity is what they prefer
and their difficulty is born of thrift.

They don't know what they are about
or even what they offer.
Are you lost? They don't try to lose you.

Don't be too hard on them (even this one).
They have an affinity with despair.
Give them long shrift.

The Poem That Does

It has started to happen
but it doesn't know it's happening
and neither, perhaps, do you

   (although the thing is happening inside you)

and even I

   (although it's travelling via my hand,
   my hand, my good left hand,
   into the scribbled words upon this page)

have no idea what it may be.
Someone handed it to me
to give to you.

What more is there to say?
Run.

About the Author

Helena Nelson's first collection (*Starlight on Water*, Rialto 2003) was a joint winner of the Jerwood Aldeburgh Prize. She went on in 2005 to found HappenStance Press, which won the Michael Marks Award for poetry publishing in 2010. Under the HappenStance imprint, she self-published two pamphlets of light verse (*Unsuitable Poems* and *The Unread Squirrel*) while also bringing out a range of books and chapbooks from over a hundred different poets. Her second collection of poems in her own right was *Plot and Counter-Plot* (Shoestring Press, 2010) and in 2016, she self-published a guide for aspiring poets: *How (Not) to Get Your Poetry Published*. In many ways, this is a companion volume.